BATS

Cindy Rodriguez

EYE to EYE
with Endangered Species

ROURKE PUBLISHING
Vero Beach, Florida 32964

© 2010 Rourke Publishing LLC

All rights reserved. No part of this book may be reproduced or utilized in any form or by any means, electronic or mechanical including photocopying, recording, or by any information storage and retrieval system without permission in writing from the publisher.

www.rourkepublishing.com

PHOTO CREDITS: Title Page: © Alexei Zaycev; 2, 3: © N Vasuki Rao; 4, 5: © Craig Dingle; 6: © Ron Hohenhaus; 6, 7, 16, 17: © Michal Krakowiak; 7: © Alexei Zaycev, Miguel Tombilla Martínez; 8: © Simon Podgorsek; 9: © Michael Rolands; 10: © U.S. Fish and Wildlife Service/ Andy King; 10, 11: © Peter Garbet; 11: © marcello mura; 12, 13 : © Styve Reineck; 14, 15: © George Burba; 17: © Photolibrary/ Nick Gordon; 18: © Alistair Scott; 18, 19: © Daniel Cooper; 19: © Eric Isselée, james steidl, rami halim; 20: © barbara miller; 20, 21: © Ryan Poling; 22: © Jan Rihak, Alexei Zaycev; 23: © Kevin Smith; 24: © Michael Lynch

Editor: Jeanne Sturm

Cover design by Teri Intzegian
Page design by Heather Botto

Library of Congress Cataloging-in-Publication Data

Rodriguez, Cindy.
 Bats / Cindy Rodriguez.
     p. cm. -- (Eye to eye with endangered species)
 Includes index.
 ISBN 978-1-60694-406-6 (hard cover)
 ISBN 978-1-60694-845-3 (soft cover)
 1. Bats--Juvenile literature. I. Title.
 QL737.C5R655 2010
 599.4--dc22

2009005997

Printed in the USA

CG/CG

Rourke Publishing

www.rourkepublishing.com - rourke@rourkepublishing.com
Post Office Box 643328 Vero Beach, Florida 32964

Table of Contents

Meet the Bat	4
A Special Mammal	6
Favorite Foods	8
Bat Babies	10
Bats are All Around!	12
Brrr...In the Winter!	14
Bat Myths	16
Watch Out! Bat Enemies	18
Help Is On the Way!	20
The Bat's Future	22
Glossary	23
Index	24

Meet the Bat

The bat is a mysterious **nocturnal** creature, and often feared. Bats lived on Earth with the dinosaurs 50 million years ago. There are more than 900 different kinds of bats. Some are very small, like the bumblebee bat, weighing less than a penny. Some are very large, like the flying fox, with a wingspan of 6 feet (2 meters).

Bats' nighttime activities provide amazing benefits. They consume countless insects and spread the seeds of tropical fruits and flowers.

Unfortunately, today about 78 species of bats are **endangered**. People may not realize many of their activities are harmful to the bat.

The grey-headed flying fox is an endangered species. It is a fruit bat that lives in Australia and is one of the largest bats in the world.

A Special Mammal

A bat is not a bird. Like all mammals, bats have fur, give birth to live babies, and nourish their young on mothers' milk.

Their wings are made of two thin layers of skin stretched over long bony fingers. The bumps, wrinkles, and flaps on their unusual faces help them find food. Bats **echolocate**, or find objects by listening to echoes.

Wildlife organizations rescue baby flying fox bats if they become separated from their mothers.

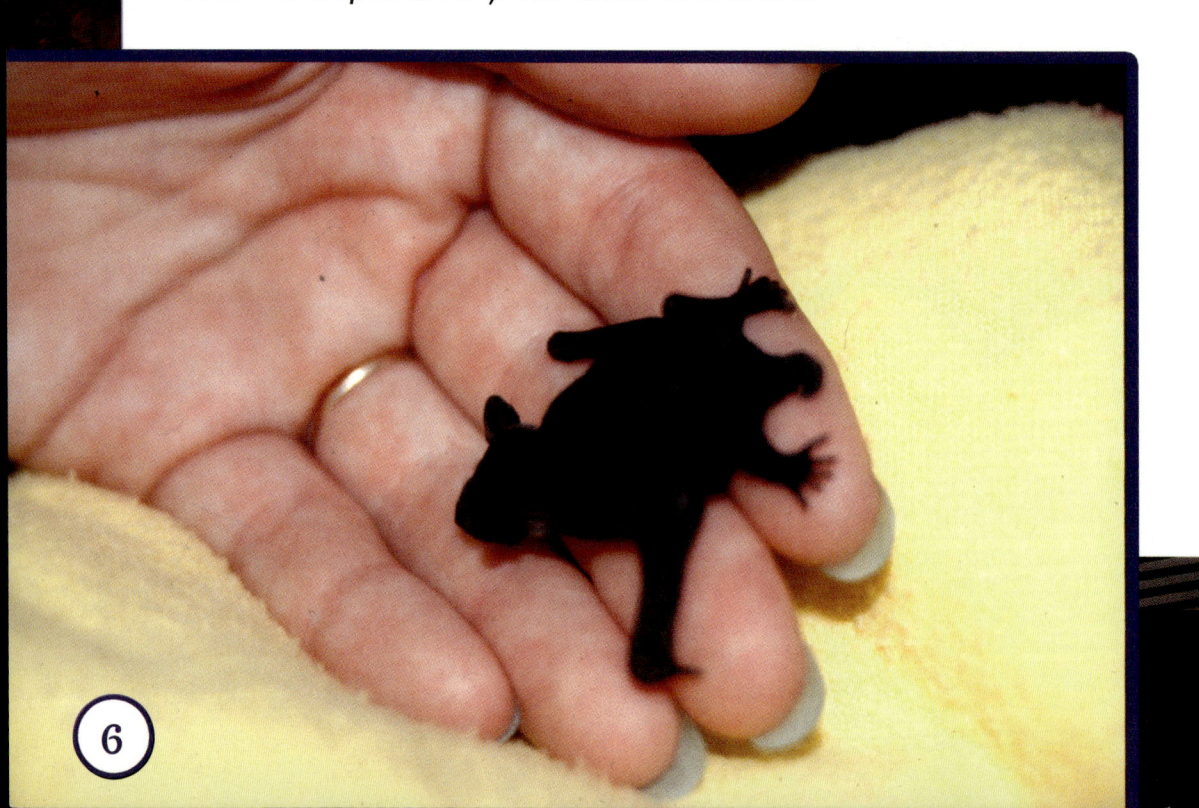

The skeletons of bats' wings are very similar to the front limbs of other mammals.

wing membrane

forearm

While not endangered, the little brown bat is very important to its environment, eating pesky insects such as mosquitoes. It is just 3.5 inches (9 centimeters) long and weighs one fourth of an ounce (7 grams)!

Favorite Foods

Bats can find their food in total darkness and eat plenty for their size. During their nighttime hunts, 70 percent of all bats eat only insects. They are **insectivores.** A little brown bat munches 600 mosquitoes in an hour. This is helpful in keeping the insect population in balance.

Some **nectivorous** bats drink nectar from flowers, and other **frugivorous** bats eat only fruit. These bats spread seeds and pollen when they **forage** through the tropical forest for food.

The Egyptian fruit bat is not endangered, but faces dangers from eating fruit grown on farms. The farmers use poison to kill the bats and keep them from destroying crops.

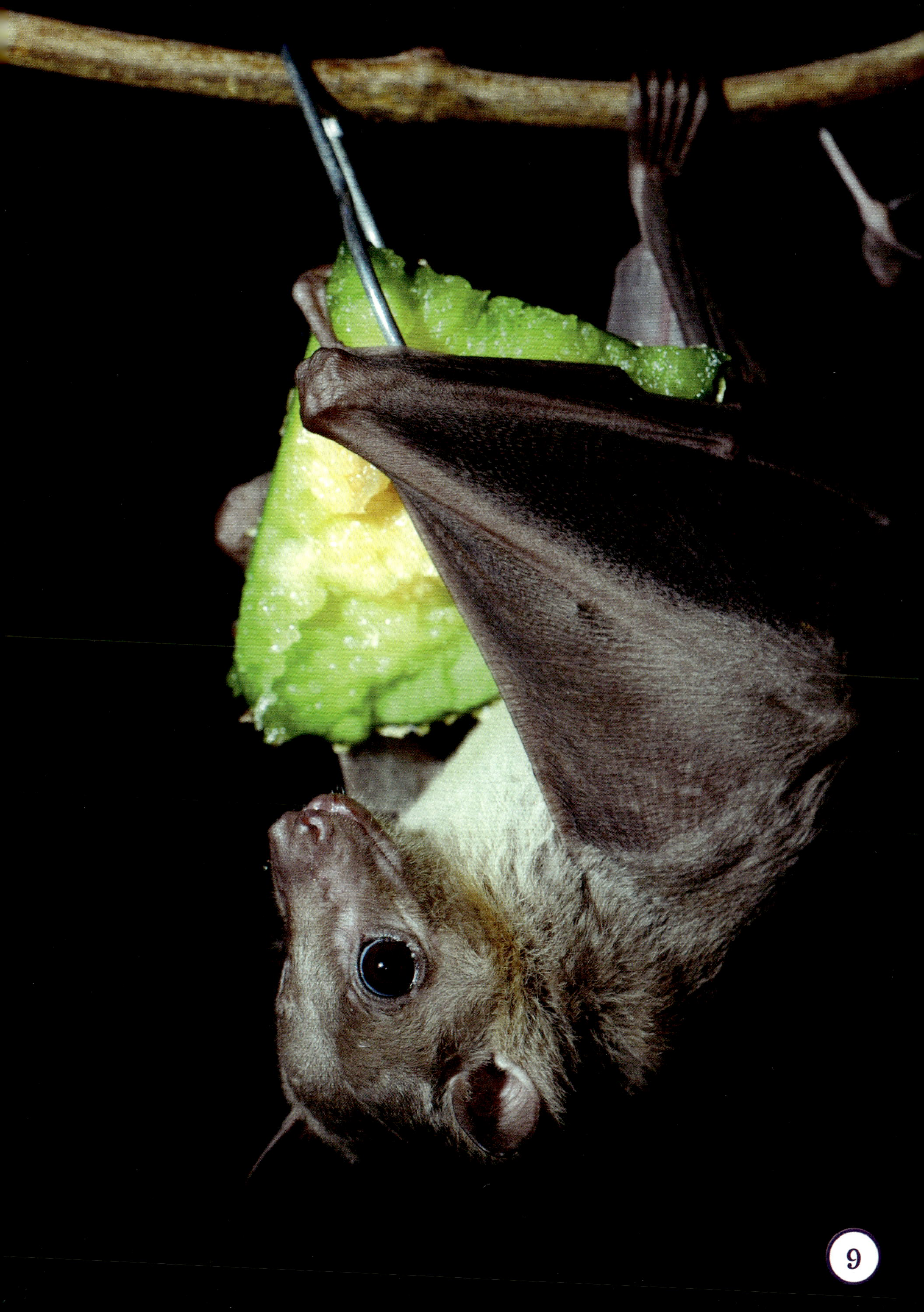

Bat Babies

Once a year in the springtime, the bat gives birth to one baby. This newborn stays with its mother for a month until it learns to fly and hunt its own food.

Groups of female bats form maternity colonies where they give birth and care for their young. These colonies are found in trees near water.

Baby bats are born blind, hairless, and defenseless.

Fun Fact

At two years old, the bat can begin to have its own babies.

Bats are All Around!

Most bats prefer a warm tropical climate, but live anywhere that is not too hot or cold. In the warmer areas, bats sleep in the same **roosts** all year. Bats either **hibernate** in the colder regions or **migrate** to hotter temperatures.

Endangered Bat Species of North America

Indiana bat
Size: 2-4 inches (51-102 millimeters) long
Weight: 0.18-0.39 ounce (5-11 grams)
Diet: flying insects
Reasons for endangered status: Indiana bats hibernate in caves. During hibernation, bats are disturbed by people exploring the caves, and killed when caves flood or collapse. Pesticide poisoning also contributes to their decline.

Greater long-nosed bat
Size: 2.75-3.75 inches (70-95 millimeters) long
Weight: 0.8-0.9 ounce (23-25 grams)
Diet: nectar, pollen, insects, and the soft fruits of cactus plants
Reasons for endangered status: Greater long-nosed bats suffer from a loss of roosts and food sources. Pesticide poisoning also contributes to their decline.

Florida bonneted bat
Size: 3.3-4.3 inches (84-109 millimeters) long
Weight: 1.2-1.7 ounces (34-48 grams)
Diet: insects, including beetles and flies
Reasons for endangered status: Florida bonneted bats' numbers are declining due to habitat loss and heavy pesticide use.

Brrr...In the Winter!

When bats remain in the colder areas, they hibernate through the months when there is little food available. Hunters and explorers may interrupt their winter's sleep and then bats will not have enough nourishment to survive.

Bats hang upside down even when they are not hibernating. Their leg muscles are not strong enough to stand for long periods of time. Most bats cannot take off flying from a standing position. Instead, they drop and glide into flight.

Fun Fact

Cave bats return every year to the same cave. Tree bats never enter caves and spend their winters inside hollow trees.

15

Bat Myths

Some myths about bats are partially responsible for many of the species that are threatened or endangered. For example, vampire bats are not endangered species, but people fear all bats because of the vampire bat's scary name.

Bats are not dirty at all, but rather very clean, like cats. Bats are not blind, either. They have good eyesight, excellent hearing, and a great sense of smell.

Another myth that threatens bats is the fear that they are aggressive and carry **rabies**. Bats are not aggressive and carry no more rabies than other wild animals.

A vampire bat does not suck blood. Instead, it pierces the flesh of horses or cattle with its sharp teeth, then catches about 2 tablespoons of blood as it comes out.

Watch Out!

Bat Enemies

Bats can live 25 to 30 years. They have a few natural **predators** like owls, snakes, raccoons, and hawks. In addition, spring floods can wash out entire caves.

Sadly, people are the bat's worst enemy. **Insecticides** poison the bat's environment and eliminate much of its food source. People often hurt bats because they fear and misunderstand this animal's behavior.

When farmers use pesticides to eliminate insects from plants, they also harm the bats that eat those bugs.

Hawk

Owl

Raccoon

Snake

Help is On the Way!

Some people recognize the importance of bats in our world. They build special houses for the bats that keep them safe and out of people's attics!

The bat house is an easy, inexpensive way for people to help bats survive their loss of a healthy habitat. Bats will return the favor by eating thousands of mosquitoes, flies, and moths around their new home.

The Anabat is an electronic ear that recognizes the bat's echolocation calls we cannot hear. This computerized detector identifies the unique sound of each bat species. This information will tell scientists where the endangered bat populations live.

The Endangered Species Act requires the United States government to identify and protect threatened bat habitats. The Anabat Bat Detector helps them achieve this goal.

The Bat's Future

Earth would be a very different place without bats. Bats control the nocturnal insect population and are the main pollinators for many flowers and fruits. They scatter seeds and replenish trees in the rain forest. Humans must learn to protect the endangered bats so they never become extinct.

Glossary

echolocate (EK-oh-loh-kate): find objects by using sound waves

endangered (en-DAYN-jurd): when a species of plant or animal is in danger of becoming extinct, or no longer living

forage (FOR-ij): look for food

frugivorous (froo-GIV-ur-uhss): animals that eat only fruit

hibernate (HYE-bur-nate): when animals spend the winter in a deep sleep

insecticides (in-SEK-tuh-sides): chemicals used to kill insects

insectivores (in-SEK-tuh-vors): animals that eat only insects

migrate (MYE-grate): when a group of animals moves from one region or climate to another

nectivorous (NEK-ti-vor-uhss): animals that eat only the nectar in flowers in the soil, water, or air

nocturnal (nok-TUR-nuhl): an animal that is active at night

predators (PRED-uh-turs): animals that live by hunting other animals for food

rabies (RAY-beez): a virus spread from the bite of an infected animal that often causes death

roosts (ROOSTS): nests or places where animals sleep

Index

Anabat 21	insect(s) 4, 8, 13, 18, 22
echolocate 6	insecticides 18
echolocation 21	mammal(s) 6, 7
endangered 4, 5, 13, 16, 21, 22	migrate 12
	myth(s) 16
food 6, 8, 10, 13, 14, 18	nocturnal 4, 22
habitat(s) 13, 20, 21	predators 18
hibernate 12, 14	roosts 12, 13

Websites to Visit

www.batcon.org/index.php/education/kids-and-education/kidz-cave.html
www.defenders.org/wildlife_and_habitat/wildlife/bats.php
www.bats4kids.org/

About the Author

Cindy Rodriguez has been teaching first graders how to read for more than 20 years. She loves using nonfiction books to involve her students in real world situations that make their reading exciting. "Caretakers of the Earth" is the motto for Cindy's school in Vero Beach, Florida, so investigating endangered species is one of her passions. She enjoys long distance running and traveling to explore new places with her two teenage daughters.